"More than anyone I know, Dr. Reese Halter manifests the wise words of Senegalese poet Baba Dioum: to save nature, we must love it; to love it, we must understand it; to understand it, we must be taught. From understanding comes wonder, which Dr. Reese is a master at evoking."

—David Perry, Professor Emeritus, Oregon State University, co-author of *Forest Ecosystems*

"*The Incomparable Honeybee*, by Dr. Reese Halter, is a wonderfully fascinating book about the almost unimaginable services honeybees (and bees in general) perform for life on Earth. Every living species fulfills a vital service for the collective good of life, whether that service is visible or not, whether we understand it or not. *The Incomparable Honeybee* is a clarion wake-up call to the fact that each time a species is lost to extinction, we are compounding the impoverishment of every generation, beginning with our own children and grandchildren."

—Chris Maser, Zoologist, author of *Earth in our Care*

"If bees had hands they would applaud Dr. Halter for his highly readable yet authoritative treatment of their lives. This vastly important but little-understood group of insects has fuelled many parts of agriculture for millennia – but fuelled it quietly, fragrantly and tastefully. Quite the contrast from our own way of being. So this book will give people pause to reflect and rejoice in the miracle of bee-dom. Let the humm continue..."

—Douglas W. Larson, Professor Emeritus, University of Guelph, author of T*he Storyteller Guitar*

The Incomparable Honeybee

The
INCOMPARABLE
Honeybee

*and the Economics
of Pollination*

Revised & Updated
Dr. Reese Halter

RMB
Victoria Vancouver Calgary

Rocky Mountain Books
www.rmbooks.com

Library and Archives Canada Cataloguing in Publication

Halter, Reese
    The incomparable honeybee and the economics of
pollination / Reese Halter. — Rev. & updated

Includes bibliographical references.
Issued also in electronic format. (ISBN 978-1-926855-65-3)
ISBN 978-1-926855-64-6

    1. Honeybee. 2. Pollination by insects.
3. Honeybee—Effect of human beings on.
4. Colony collapse disorder of honeybees. I. Title.

QL568.A6H34 2011   595.79'9   C2011-903303-8

Printed and bound in Canada

Rocky Mountain Books acknowledges the financial support for its publishing program from the Government of Canada through the Canada Book Fund (CBF) and the Canada Council for the Arts, and from the province of British Columbia through the British Columbia Arts Council and the Book Publishing Tax Credit.

 Canadian Heritage Patrimoine canadien Canada Council for the Arts Conseil des Arts du Canada

 BRITISH COLUMBIA ARTS COUNCIL

The interior pages of this book have been produced on 100% post-consumer recycled paper, processed chlorine free and printed with vegetable-based dyes.

MIX
Paper from
responsible sources
FSC® C016245

For my mentor and hero:
my Dad, Aubrey J. Halter (1918–2008)

Contents

A Story of Reciprocation

This is a story about the most important pollinators on Earth – the remarkable bees. I cannot tell the bees' story in isolation, though, as it interweaves with those of humans and many ecological systems on our planet. The interreliant relationships these little creatures maintain are cause for great celebration and, currently, great concern. Over the past *four* years, a staggering number of bees have died – over 250 billion. This sad fact lends itself to an imperative discussion, one in which we increase our understanding of the reciprocation that is necessary to improve the health of bees, humans and our planet as a whole. With this enhanced knowledge, we must then take action to protect the remaining species of bees from extinction.

The story of the first bees began at least 100 million years ago – thus, it's a story 14 times older than that of the first human progenitors. Currently, there are approximately 20,000 named species of bees and perhaps as many as 40,000 kinds of bees worldwide. In North America alone – from the bitter cold of the Arctic Circle to the furnace-like Sonoran Desert – there are over 5,000 native species. No matter where in the world, regional plant life and bees have exquisitely adapted to flourish *together* in their specific environments.

To reproduce, flowers need bees to carry pollen from one to another – cross-pollination. Bees need the protein-rich pollen and vitamin-rich nectar from flowers for their reproductive processes, which vary in complexity between species. For instance, the most straightforward practice is that of the solitary bee species – the majority of bees worldwide. Solitary bees lay one egg in a nest often lined with overlapping pink, yellow, blue and purple petals packed with digested pollen and honey – a mix of dehydrated nectar with special bee ingredients – then seal the hole and move on.

Honey, bumble and stingless bees, on the other hand, are social insects. Each bee has a specific role in a complex process of reproduction. Orchestration and co-operation are required, among a couple of hundred bees in the annual bumble bees to more than several thousand in stingless bees. Honeybees – our primary focus here – collaborate in colonies as large as 100,000 insects, in which one queen and many female workers govern. Intricate communication enables each colony to continuously respond to changing environmental factors. For example, the honeybees perform elaborate dances to detail and pinpoint newly discovered sources of food.

From honey hunters to the current wave of urban beekeepers, humans have also long appreciated the taste and health benefits of honey. For over 5,000 years, humans have kept honeybees in artificial hives. In fact, the oldest known apiary is 3,000 years old and was recently found in the Iron Age city of Tel Rehov in Israel. The bees that were kept there most likely originated from Turkey, hundreds of kilometres away. Efficient storage, however, did not become available until 1851, when Reverend Lorenzo Langstroth, in Massachusetts, improved upon various European hive techniques and invented the perfect beekeeper hive. Consisting of two or three storeys with removable rectangular wooden frames, the Langstroth hive enables bees to build honeycomb and store honey in a suitable artificial environment.

Producing honey is not the only way honey-bees contribute to human society, though. From the multi-use marvel of beeswax to potentially detecting and treating disease, the gifts humans receive from honeybees are phenomenal.

Often unknowingly, we are dependent on bees to do much more than produce goods of the hive. Bees pollinate over 110 crops in North America (and elsewhere). Economically, the total value of all bees' work, or what scientists now call ecosystem services, is at least $3-billion in Canada, $44-billion in the US and $2.3-billion in Australia. This fact is even more thought-provoking if you consider what would happen if there were few of these species left. From fruits and vegetables to crops that support the beef and dairy industries, we rely on bees to pollinate over one-third of everything on our plates at meal-time. Beyond that, the cotton fields that lend part of their harvests to textile production also require these savvy pollinators. Unfortunately, agriculture as currently practised works against the natural environment and against the bees.

Despite this endless generosity of bees, humans have neglected their own role in this fragile relationship. Honeybees and humans share many similarities: we socialize, dance, eat honey, touch, feel, mimic one another, sleep, enjoy caffeine and nicotine, vote, and get sick. But in recent years, bees' autoimmune systems have been shutting down and bee colonies have been collapsing. There is no single reason for this. Scientists believe it is instead a combination of biological and environmental factors, mass over-use of synthetic toxins and our antiquated agricultural system that are the culprits.

Bees are capable of helping humans when we fall ill, and they provide for us at all times. In turn, we need to renew our commitment to this relationship. A tremendous amount is at stake. In March of 2011 the United Nations issued a warning that mass bee deaths signal the writing on the wall for global food security. Until we properly reciprocate, we move closer toward eventual eradication of the bees, thus jeopardizing our own health and life as we know it on this planet.

As an intelligent, problem-solving species, we humans have choices to make. It is simply unacceptable that we allow the destruction of an estimated one species every 20 minutes of every day of every year. We must harness the hope that exists and foster the waves of change. To do this, we need to inform ourselves on the current situation and risks, understand what actions we can take as individuals and take action in every way possible. Understanding our interweaving stories is a first step in this right direction.

In the Beeginning

The history of bees begins with the evolution of plant life. While life on our planet began over 3.5 billion years ago, land plants have been around for about 400 million years. Giant horsetails, ferns, cycads and conifers – trees that bear cones and release naked seeds, such as pines and redwoods – all relied upon the wind to disseminate male pollen and assist in cross-pollinating plants. The prehistoric forests were so prolific that the billions of tons of organic matter accumulated in the Carboniferous Period – 354 to 290 million years ago – currently provides fossil fuels to most of humankind.

At the beginning of the Cretaceous Period – about 140 million years ago – land plants underwent a fantastic change. They grew colourful, pungent flowers filled with large, protein-rich pollen grains surrounded by nectar. Instead of relying on the wind to cross-pollinate these new flowering plants (angiosperms), nature conscripted insects – initially beetles and flies – by enticing them with the sweet and nutritious nectar. While feeding, these insects inadvertently brush against the male anther and transfer its pollen to an adjacent flower's receptive female stigma. The pollen fertilizes the ovule, which develops into a seed. Eventually, a fruit grows to enclose the seed(s).

By the end of the Cretaceous – about 65 million years ago – the diversity of plant life had exploded, adding over 21,000 angiosperms to about 3,000 species of conifers. Today, there are over 235,000 different species of angiosperms catalogued, whereas there are only 650 kinds of conifers remaining. Geologic upheavals and climate change have certainly had a hand in this change, but one particular insect has irrefutably assisted the angiosperms in conquering the land: bees. While flies, gnats, beetles, butterflies, moths, hummingbirds and bats are pollinators too, bees conduct the lion's share of pollinating on Earth today.

The first bees evolved from predatory wasps

about 100 million years ago. Bees specialized in feeding on the sweet carbohydrate nectar as a high energy source, which they eventually convert into honey. They also collect pollen as their only source of protein – a requisite for the development of offspring. When the bee lands on a flower, hairs of the positively charged bee attract the negatively charged pollen. This electrostatic charge is what enables most bees to be efficient pollinators. However, some workers deliberately make small packets of pollen using their saliva and store them inside the sidesaddle pouches on their hind legs – pollen baskets. Later, moving around inside another flower, bees unintentionally touch the female's stigma and pollinate it. None the wiser, they move on and continue their own quest for resources.

This interdependent relationship between flowering plants and their golden-haired pollination partners has grown ever more exclusive over time. For instance, the architecture of many flowers has adapted to allow only a bee's tongue to access the nectar. Most species of bees have subsequently witnessed a lengthening of their tongues over time.

The visible world is very different for bees, as they cannot see red but can detect ultraviolet (UV) light. Their unique visible spectrum grants bees access to a vibrant world in which some flowers that appear as one colour to humans actually have a much more intricate and colourful design. Almond flowers, for instance, use a neon colour visible only to bees, which guides the bees to receptive flowers.

Plants have also developed ingenious signals to inform pollinators when pollination has occurred. Many plant species use pungent floral scents to attract pollinators. Once pollinated, their scent dissipates. Some, like the vanilla orchid flower, fold up and appear desiccated within a half hour of pollination. Other flowers change colour once pollinated.

Native Bees of North America

The intimate relationship between bees and plants has thus far – mostly – served to ensure the survival of both. No matter what the geographical region, each species of plant and bee has adapted to the specific climate and characteristics of the area. Before we begin our specific discussion of honeybees, I want to take a moment to recognize other remarkable species of bees that brave the environment of North America, specifically the Great Plains Grassland.

The Great Plains Grassland occupies an astoundingly vast area of central North America, encompassing 14 per cent of the total area of Canada and the US. The story of this prairie land is one that revolves around climate. A land of extremes, the prairies are either inundated by glacial meltwater or dry as a bone. A vast and hardy assemblage of more than 2,000 species of plants and animals are native to the prairies. Almost 70 per cent of these plants depend upon various species of solitary and bumble bees to assist them with cross-pollination.

In fact, nearly 25 per cent of the native plants on the Great Plains Grassland have evolved *with* specific species of native bumble bees. In Missouri, for example, the long-tongued black and yellow bumble bee (*Bombus nevadensis*) services – almost exclusively – the wild bergamot plant. The eastern bumble bee (*Bombus impatiens*) cross-pollinates only the spikes of Culver's root with its specially adapted short tongue. Solitary bees too have formed almost exclusive relationships with some crop plants. For instance, the squash and gourd bees mate, sleep and dine on their respectively named plants. I have seen pumpkin bees chewing their way out of a wilted flower in the morning in order to get to the next open flower. Two species of solitary bees, the alkali bee (*Nomia melanderi*) and the alfalfa bee (*Megachile pacifica*), are con-scripted in commercial alfalfa seed production, which then feeds millions of cattle.

Distinctions between honey, bumble and solitary bees often seem blurred to the untrained eye, but the unique characteristics of each are vital for pollinating different types of plants. For instance, whereas honeybees drink nectar from the side of some plants, solitary and bumble bees will snap open the floral heads and exchange pollen while they sip on the nectar. However, bumble bees also are known "nectar robbers" because they sometimes tear a hole in the corolla (all the petals) of a flower to extract the nectar. Whenever this larcenous activity occurs, the bee fails to trip the flower's pollination mechanism. Thus, no seeds are set and the flower must wait for a more obedient bee – perhaps of a different species – to happen along.

Several factors are currently threatening the native bees of North America. While I will address these issues farther on, for now I want to plant a few seeds of thought. As you continue reading, perhaps begin to think about how each of these issues is harmful to bee populations. For starters, climate change is affecting the timing, or phenology, of plant flowering, which is often occurring earlier in the season. Destruction of natural habitat has been rampant in recent decades, as has widespread application of synthetic herbicides and pesticides. All these things are having a deleterious effect on our native bees.

Not only do these factors harm bee populations, but many species are actually being wiped out altogether. Limiting the consideration only to species of bumble bees, the list – so far – is grim. Since 1999, the rusty-patched bumble bee (*Bombus affinis*) – whose habitat spanned from Quebec to Vermont – has disappeared. Franklin's bumble bee (*Bombus franklini*) of northern California and southern Oregon is also now believed to be extinct. The once large population of the western bumble bee (*Bombus occidentalis*), which inhabited the entire west coast of North America – from Alaska to California – has severely declined, as have the American bumble bee (*Bombus pennsylvanicus*) and the yellow-banded bumble bee (*Bombus terricola*), by as much as 96 per cent. The geographic ranges of these species have contracted by between 23 per cent and 87 per cent, some within just the past two decades. The latter three bumble bees have also exhibited high infection levels of the pathogen called *Nosema bombi* and they displayed less genetic diversity than other bumble bee populations that were not in decline. The *Nosema bombi* parasite germinates in the gut and destroys the digestive system. It's commonly found in bumble bees throughout Europe but until now has been largely unstudied in North America; at this moment it remains unclear whether this parasite was introduced from Europe to North America.

Bumble Bees

We all know the title of this manifesto is *The Incomparable Honeybee*, so why is this section about bumble bees? Well, my reasoning is two-fold. First, all species of bees are important in a multitude of ways. That said, having knowledge of another type of bee enhances the ability to appreciate the matchlessly complex society and behaviour of the honeybees. Through comparison, we see how the honeybees are truly incomparable. So, let's take a quick look at the life cycle and attributes of the bumble bee.

There are about 60 species of North American bumble bees in which each individual weighs an average of half a gram, or at least two-and-a-half times more than a queen honeybee. Although a colony of bumble bees may visit a wide variety of flowers during the course of a season, an individual bee visits only one species of plant on a single trip away from the nest. Bumble bees visit two to three times more flowers than honeybees during a 15-hour workday. Despite living in colonies – like honeybees – bumble bees do not have an intricate system of communication. Rather, they work in solitude, tirelessly starting before dawn and often finishing after sunset in cool and sometimes inhospitable environs.

Recent research conducted at Queen Mary University in London shows that bumble bees in the UK can find the solution to a complex mathematical problem that keeps computers busy for days. Although their brains may be the size of a pinhead, bumble bees show advanced cognitive capacities with very limited numbers of neurons. Moreover, bumble bees are able to find the shortest distance between each nectar and pollen patch, effectively solving the age-old question that the travelling salesman constantly grapples with: how to find the shortest path that allows him to visit all locations on his route.

Today we are one step closer to understanding how bumble bee brains work because of groundbreaking research conducted by 28 British schoolchildren aged 8 to 10 who discovered that buff-tailed bumble bees (*Bombus terrestris*) use a combination of colours and spatial relationships in deciding which colour of flower to forage from. The students' project was even reported in the prestigious peer-reviewed Royal Society journal *Biology Letters*.

While most bees are proficient pollinators, bumble and some solitary bees perform an even more astounding fertilization feat called buzz pollination, or sonification. Buzz pollination entails a bee grabbing hold of a flower and curling up her abdomen – the rearward segments of a bee that contain its digestive and reproductive organs – to form a c shape. Closing her wings over her thorax, or midsection, the bee shivers her strong flight muscles to create a sonic vibration. This robust vibration shakes the flower and, importantly, the male anthers, where the pollen is stored. A copious amount of pollen dislodges from the anthers and coats the bee by means of the electrostatic attraction. The bee then grooms and moves on to continue foraging; invariably, pollen reaches the female stigma of another flower. Pollination accomplished!

These bees' magnificent sonification technique

is responsible for the pollination of – to name only a few – sunflowers, canola, rapeseed, raspberries, strawberries, blackberries, lentils, peas, tomatoes, chilies, red clover, alfalfa and all species of potato, worldwide. Commercial greenhouses have tried tools such as electric vibration wands to replicate buzz pollination by bees, but such manual pollination techniques increase costs and produce significantly lower yields. In Australia the lack of native bumble bees on the mainland posed a challenge for interested parties such as greenhouse growers. Efforts to import bumble bees were resisted due to past issues with non-native species in the country, so researchers began focusing instead on native species – blue-banded bees – that are capable of similar sonification. With more than 8 per cent of the 235,000 flowering plant species in the world relying on the unique buzz pollination technique to reproduce, the importance of bumble and solitary bees is clear.

These prodigious workers are able to fly in snowstorms, wind and rain at 11–20 kilometres per hour (7 to 12 miles per hour). Even when a bumble bee has two full pollen baskets, which add about 20 per cent more weight, or 100 milligrams, to its body – it can fly as far as 6 kilometres (3.7 miles) from the nest. The bumble bee uses the same aerodynamic principle as helicopters with reverse-pitch semi-rotary blades do: each time a bumble bee's wings swing back and forth (one oscillation cycle), a type of cavity or vacuum is produced in the air above the wing. This cavity provides extra lift for the large bumble bee and her load of pollen.

A bumble bee, however, cannot lift off unless her body is warmer than 35°C (95°F). If she lives at the frigid Arctic Circle – for instance – the only possible food source that could give her enough energy is honey. In fact, it takes a honey-fuelled bumble bee only seconds to rev up her body temperature from 20°C (68°F) to 35°C – an extraordinary achievement accomplished by shivering her musculature. On the other hand, if a bumble bee's body temperature exceeds 44°C (111°F) it uses its abdomen to transfer heat and cool off.

The defence behaviour of bumble bees is not seen in either stingless or honeybees. Despite seeming rather docile, a bumble bee will raise her middle legs when she is bothered while mildly at rest or perched. If further annoyed, the bumble bee will roll on her back, brace her body and point her stinger while opening her mouth. Since bumble bees do not have barbed stingers, they are able to sting repeatedly. Predators – like skunks, shrikes and foxes – receive extra treatment, as bumble bees spray feces and vomit honey on them.

Typically, a colony of bumble bees is annual. Each spring, the queen bumble bee emerges from her eight-month hibernation. Upon waking, her first order of business is to find flowers to provide her with nectar and pollen. Inseminated the previous fall, she also collects pollen to fertilize her first eggs. Using grasses or the inside of an old mouse den, she builds a nest. From her wax gland, the queen makes a small honey pot and regurgitates the nectar into it. After laying eight to ten eggs in the nest, the queen covers it with a waxen canopy that, despite the chilly spring air, maintains a temperature of 30°C (86°F). The queen then sits on the brood – much like a hen – and sips from the honey pot all night long.

In the morning, she breaks the waxen nest cover and shivers to warm her body up to 35°C. She then darts off to collect more honey and pollen. After three days, the eggs hatch. The queen feeds these new female workers honey and pollen for the next 16 to 25 days, after which they are mature. During their meagre two weeks of life after maturation, these bees are responsible for collecting nectar and pollen, making wax pots and helping with second-generation eggs. The queen's last batch of eggs produces approximately 100 queens and 100 drones. At the end of the season, the queen dies. The process begins again with a new queen that emerges in the last batch of eggs.

The life expectancy of a colony of bumble bees – usually with a population of no more than 400 individuals – depends on the length of the growing season. For instance, queen bumble bees that live at the Arctic Circle – where the growing season is relatively short – emerge at 0°C (32°F) and live for no longer than two-and-a-half months. Conversely, in Central and South America, some bumble bee species can live for up to two years and colonies can reach a population of 2,000 individuals.

The Complex Society of Honeybees

While the majority of bees worldwide are solitary or have colonies of independent workers, honeybees co-operate in a complex society within their colony or hive. The hive can contain as many as 100,000 individuals, but one queen bee rules the colony by constantly emitting at least 18 pheromones, or hormones.

Under the queen's rule, a highly efficient organization exists in which all members work for the common good. The workers in the hive are all females, with only about 200 to 300 males, or drones, at any one time during the summer months. The queen, workers and drones have different roles to play. While the queen and the drones maintain one function from birth, worker bees progress through a series of different responsibilities.

The body of a honeybee consists of a series of

hardened plates covered with dense hairs. Most of its vital organs – including the venomous barbed stinger – are inside the bee's abdomen. It has a head with three smaller eyes that detect polarized light, enabling bees to use the sun as a compass. Two larger, hairy, compound eyes help determine wind flow and colours – including UV radiation, violet blue, blue green, green yellow and orange, but not red. A worker bee's head has two antennae loaded with 3,000 sensory organs. Their ability to distinguish more than 170 odours is vital for smelling nectar, pollen, water, tree resin and alert pheromones.

The honeybee's midsection, or thorax, has three pairs of legs and two sets of wings. The six hairy legs are important for walking, prying flowers open, dancing on the comb and grooming. The hind legs contain pollen baskets, or corbicula. The two pairs of wings beat at 200 cycles per second and defy the rules of aerodynamics in their masterful ability to allow a honeybee to travel at speeds greater than 24 kilometres per hour (15 miles per hour) for up to 13 kilometres (8 miles) at a time. During flight, the honeybee is able to maintain a thorax temperature of an astonishing 46°C (115°F) by passing the excess heat to its head by regurgitating droplets of watered-down honey, cooling the head off just as sweat does in mammals.

The queen makes piping sounds and lays about 1,500 eggs per day, or between 175,000 and 200,000 per year. Normally, she is able to perform her role for about four years. Six to ten young bees, usually less than 12 days old, surround her. They constantly examine the queen with their antennae and forelegs while licking her with their hairy tongues. After the queen lays about 30 eggs, they feed and groom her and remove her feces. The queen's retinue manufactures a protein- and lipid-rich royal jelly from two different sets of glands in their heads, which they pass to the queen in a direct mouth-to-mouth action. Royal jelly contains vitellogenin, an indispensable protein that boosts the immune defence system, reduces stress and acts as a potent antioxidant to help reduce wear and tear throughout the queen's body.

After three days, the eggs hatch. Young bees, known as nurse bees, feed the larvae royal jelly – analogous to mother's milk – for three days. After that, the nurse bees feed the larvae a mixture of pollen and honey called bees' bread. Bees' bread contains lactic acid bacteria that ferment the pollen to make it more nutritious, digestible and mould-resistant than raw pollen. By the seventh day of feeding, the larvae have increased their weight 500-fold since birth. If this occurred in humans, the average newborn baby would weigh 1,360 kilograms (or a ton and a half!).

On the ninth day of their life cycle, the larvae finish eating and spin a cocoon. The nurse bees make a wax in their abdomen to cap the hexagonal cocoon cell and enable the larvae to complete their development. Twenty-one days later, the larvae have become worker bees and they chew through the waxen cell cap, emerge and immediately begin to clean their cell. With the assistance of 15 to 30 workers, one cell takes a bee, on average, 41 minutes to prepare. The vitality of the colony relies on this process, as the queen will only lay eggs in cells that are clean.

Drones – born in late summer – emerge after 24 days. Nurse bees must feed them for about a week, but after that they must provide for themselves. These male bees are larger than workers but smaller than queens, and do not possess stingers. Drones have only one role in the colony, which most never fulfill: to inseminate virgin queens. Their eyes are very large and their antennae are ten times more sensitive than worker bees', each equipped with 30,000 sensory receptors especially adapted for smelling virginal queens. For the duration of their three-week lives, they exit the hive at midday and congregate with drones from different colonies before returning in late afternoon.

From a very young age, the worker honey-bee has a phenomenal ability to multi-task. Throughout her life – of less than 60 days – she may perform as many as 20 tasks. For instance, a young bee will tend to the nursery, clean brood cells, patrol the hive on sanitation duty and assist at capping the comb. Capping one comb takes six hours and hundreds of workers. Before a young bee graduates to one of the most remarkable (and not yet fully understood) feats of nature – the perfect construction of a honey-comb – she will greet an older forager bee. The forager stores nectar collected from flowers in a special compartment in her abdomen called the honey crop. She returns to the hive and passes the nectar along to – usually – three young receiving bees.

The nectar is comprised mostly of water and as much as 20 per cent sugar. The receiver bee moves to a less crowded area of the hive and repeatedly folds and unfolds her mouthparts, exposing the nectar to air to evaporate the water. At the same time, she secretes the enzyme invertase to help transform the nectar into honey. She then places the dehydrated nectar into a cell to further reduce the water content below 18 per cent. Other worker bees fan the open cells at 24,500 wing-beats per minute. After a couple of days, the nectar is now honey and ready to be sealed or capped in the cell.

Honey, with its high caloric energy, is the fuel of the hive. One kilogram (2.2 pounds) contains about 3,250 calories. Compared to the same weight of apples (400 calories), oranges (230) or cucumbers (140), honey is essentially rocket fuel. One teaspoon of honey weighing 21 grams contains 16 grams of sugar, or 60 calories. It takes 12 honeybees a combined flying distance of over 9,600 kilometres (5,965 miles) – and their entire foraging lives – to produce that 21 grams of honey. Worldwide, the species of honeybee that is the Clydesdale workhorse of honeymaking is the Italian honeybee (*Apis mellifera*).

Colonies store much more nectar than pollen. Pollen contains between 6 and 20 per cent protein and is vital for the growing young of the colony. It takes 15 to 50 kilograms (33 to 110 pounds) of pollen a year – compared to 60 to 80 kilograms (132 and 176 pounds) of honey – to maintain a hive for one year. This translates into one million trips for pollen and four million trips for nectar by foraging bees. Some forager workers unload pollen baskets to young receiver workers, who in turn treat the pollen with a phytocidal acid to prevent germination. This treatment enables the pollen to be mixed with honey as bees' bread capped in cells.

It takes 66,000 bee-hours of activity to produce the 77,000 splendid hexagonal cells that form the comb of the hive. Almost 9 kilograms (20 pounds) of honey are required for a young worker bee to produce one kilogram (2.2 pounds) of beeswax. Bees eat the honey and trigger a gland in their abdomen to secrete wax. The bees then chew the wax flakes to soften them. One kilogram of this hearty wax can support 22 kilograms (48 pounds) of honey, or more than 20 times its own weight. Many decades ago, the aeronautics industry recognized the strength of honeycomb and adapted nature's design to enhance the bending and stiffness of aircraft wings, as the wings must support heavy loads of fuel in the aircraft.

To construct the honeycomb, hair plates at the base of a bee's neck act as a plumb bob to determine the changing orientation to gravity. When a worker bee turns relative to the Earth's gravitational field, the pressure of the hair plates on its legs tells the bee which way is up. Without these hair plates, workers could not build honeycomb. When honeybees were transported into outer space on the 1984 Challenger shuttle flight, they were unable to construct honeycomb, due to the lack of gravitational force.

Workers use the tips of their antennae to assess the thickness and smoothness of comb cells, but the exactness of the cell diameters and their orientation is still not explained. Bees construct honeycomb horizontally. Amazingly, chambers are back to back at exactly a 13-degree angle to prevent honey from dripping out.

Propolis is the glue that bees use to cement and enhance the strength of the comb base. They also extensively coat the entire hive nest cavity with a thin waterproofing and insulating antifungal and antibacterial layer. To make propolis, bees combine enzymes from their mouths with the pollen, nectar, water and tree resin. Propolis also patches holes, prevents ants from invading and embalms intruders that are too large for the bees to remove from the hive. If a mouse enters the hive, the bees sting it to death and use propolis to mummify it, therefore protecting the colony from bacteria that would otherwise flourish on the dead rodent.

Within the comb, storage and space allocation is meticulous. Storing honey near the points where the comb attaches minimizes the potential stress that such a heavy substance could cause to the wax comb at the top of the hive. The nursery is located in cells that allow maintenance of the temperature in the central part of the comb. Larger drone cells take space along the comb edges.

Honeybees are extremely hygienic. About 1 per cent of all workers are constantly on sanitation duty, removing mouldy pollen, old cell caps, dead workers or deadbeat drones.

After young comb-building workers graduate, their first job outside is to provide a fan or exhaust system for the hive. Hundreds of bees work just outside the hive entrance by fanning their wings at 24,500 beats a minute to help cool the colony and remove carbon dioxide. When the colony temperature exceeds 35°C (95°F), forager bees bring loads of water into the hive and pass them to receiver bees. The receiver bees tongue-lash the water onto developing eggs and honeycomb while nurse bees fan their wings to create an ingenious evaporative cooling system.

Fanning bees later graduate to become guard bees. As the name implies, they patrol outside the hive and closely scrutinize every forager bee upon its arrival back at the hive. Guard bees stand on their back four legs with antennae held forward and forelegs lifted. They ascertain the odour and behaviour of every bee entering. If they detect trouble, they emit an alarm pheromone that quickly signals a red alert. When honey hunters and beekeepers use smoke on a hive, it is to dilute this pheromone.

Worker bees have barbed stingers that detach from their abdomens but continue to inject venom into victims for up to one minute. A furious honeybee will sting in the same place repeatedly. The stinger is a honeybee's main source of defence. Once it is released, she dies.

About 25 per cent of the colony workers are forager bees, the oldest workers. They average 10 to 15 trips a day, but as many as 150 trips are possible. Visiting between one and one thousand flowers of the same species in a day, a one-way trip can be as far as 13 kilometres (8 miles). Forager bees work themselves to death, as after 800 kilometres (497 miles) their bodies simply stop functioning. If there are crosswinds upon exiting the hive, honeybees turn their bodies indirectly into the wind to minimize resistance and economize on honey consumption. To return to the hive, they may use a number of landmarks such as trees, rock formations or barns to help guide them.

Thirty five per cent of the foragers are scout bees, constantly on the lookout for new sources of nectar, pollen, tree resin and water. Scouts are also responsible for identifying a new location for the hive when it is time to swarm. When the strength of the queen's pheromones diminishes, nurse bees feed about half a dozen larvae only royal jelly as they begin to rear a new queen. In the meantime, scout bees find a new location. They reach a consensus on a new location by voting. Research has shown that 15 is the crucial number of scout bees for a quorum. Then they wait for the signal to evacuate.

Taking about half of the colony with her, the reigning queen travels in the centre of the swarm. It takes about 40 days for the bees to build a new hive. Timing is very important, as in most cases there are not enough flowers in bloom for a late summer swarm to successfully build comb and have enough stored honey to last the winter.

Meanwhile, back at the old hive the first new queen to hatch has a pressing task to complete: to murder all competing soon-to-be-emerging queens. Once she has secured her position, she undertakes her only flight out of the nest. Releasing as little as a billionth of a gram of her scent, she attracts drones. The queen may mate with a couple dozen drones, storing as much as seven million sperm – enough to last her a life-time. The drones take three seconds to ejaculate before their penis is ripped out of their body, after which – writhing in pain – they die.

The last batch of bees to hatch before winter must gorge themselves on protein- and lipid-rich pollen-based bees' bread. The protein enables them to store vitellogenin in their bodies so they can provide royal jelly to the queen and her first eggs that hatch in the springtime.

About a quarter of the bees in a hive over winter are constantly shivering and moving in a concentric circle around the queen. Similar to the emperor penguins of the South Pole, they utilize the warmth of the thermal mass. Every bee takes turns in the warmest central part of the circular mass, as those on the outside repeatedly shuffle into the centre and then back out to the exterior. The temperature in the hive never drops below 18°C (64°F).

Intricate Steps of Communication

Communication among bees varies by species. For example, the meliponine stingless bees communicate with one another by transmitting sound signals. Duration and frequencies of these sounds translate into information about distances to new food, water and tree resin sources.

In order for a social society like honeybees to thrive, they must also constantly communicate new information about the colony and its current requirements. Honeybees communicate by dancing. Each performed dance taps into the amazing ability honeybees possess to rapidly switch foraging tasks based on the immediate needs of the hive. Up-to-date information dictates whether worker bees are to forage for nectar, pollen, water or tree resin.

Nobel laureate Karl von Frisch (1886–1982) dedicated his life to unravelling many of the mysteries of the honeybee. He was the first researcher to decipher the purposeful and endearing dancing of bees. Decades of subsequent research revealed four primary dances: the *round*, *c-shaped*, *waggle* and *vibrational* dances, and at least five other, less-understood dances. While sometimes performed outside on the surface of the swarm, dances are more likely to happen inside the hive, near the entrance on the vertical comb or farther inside in total darkness. In the latter case, the bees rely on their acute senses of smell, taste and touch to interpret the dance.

When a scout or forager bee finds a rich blossom patch, it sips every drop of nectar from deep within the flower, using her long, hairy, straw-like tongue, or glossa. Then she turns her scent pocket inside out, saturating it with the pungent floral aroma. The scent pocket is a damp, glistening pad tucked inside a small fold of skin near the tip of a bee's tail.

When the excited worker arrives back at the hive, she finds usually three receiver bees to off-load most of the nectar. She then performs a dance indicating the new source of nectar. If the blossoms are within 10 metres (33 feet) of the hive, the bee performs the *round* dance. First, she will exchange a few drops of nectar so the other bees can taste it. Then she starts spinning around in a narrow circle, changing direction to the right and then the left, dancing one or two circles in each direction.

Other bees follow the dancer very closely. Their antennae touch and smell her scent gland and thousands of her hairs containing nectar residue. Twenty or more dance cycles can take place, with the dances lasting between a few seconds and a minute. The longer the dance, the more workers she recruits.

If the nectar is between 10 and 100 metres (33 and 328 feet) from the hive, the scout will perform a *c-shaped* dance. This dance is quite similar to the round dance, except, of course, the scout never completes an entire circle. The c-shaped and round dances do not give workers an exact nectar location. Rather, they communicate that the bounty is within close proximity of the hive. Bees' powerful sense of smell may then guide them to the new floral source.

The *waggle* dance is one of the most extraordinary forms of communication in the entire animal kingdom. This dance conveys precise information about the food's location, including its direction and the distance from the hive – as far as 13 kilometres (8 miles). In his research, von Frisch determined that workers assess critical fragments of information from each of the dance's components, including the duration of waggling and buzzing; the length of the straight run, in comb cell diameters; the number of unit circuits per dance; and the average distance of the dances from the hive entrance.

The waggle dance follows a nearly figure-eight shape, but with a straight (bee)line connecting the two semicircles. The scout runs along a narrow semicircle, making sharp turns, and then beelines straight back to her starting point. She then performs the same moves in the opposite direction. The dance is elaborate, with the bee waggling her abdomen in precise, intricate steps. At each turn she vigorously shakes her body: the side to side waggle occurs about 13 to 15 times a second and gives off a buzzing sound as her muscles and skeleton vibrate.

At the end of a complete dance, the scout will stop and share nectar with other workers, who extend their antennae to smell the dancer. Some new followers even squeak, causing the dancer to stop midstream and feed them a droplet of nectar.

Dance tempo and beeline length indicate distance from the hive to the flowers. That is, followers assess the distance by measuring the number of circuits per 15 seconds and the amount of time spent waggling and buzzing on the straight run. A slow dance tempo and long straight run communicate that the distance is greater. It does not convey exact distance, but informs the other bees of the amount of energy needed to find the new resource. This translates into the amount of honey each forager must eat before leaving the hive. The waggle dance can also inform foragers about new sources of water, tree resin and pollen.

The extent of the waggling, the total number of dance cycles and the intensity of the buzzing vibrations all work together to communicate the quality of the flowers at the new source. The richer the nectar, the greater the intensity of these three attributes. The longer an entire waggle dance sequence is, the larger the size of the floral patch.

Fascinatingly, the waggle dance – mostly performed in the dark and on the vertical face of the comb – somehow conveys the horizontal direction to the food source. Research suggests that if the dancer's beelines move straight up the hive wall, foragers should fly toward the sun to find the source. Running straight down the wall means they must fly away from the sun. Amazingly, the dancer will match the movement of the sun during the dance by modifying the angle of the beeline.

Specialized organs at the base of a bee's neck are able to detect the gravitational angle of the dance and translate this information into the angle of the sun to the horizon. When bees exit the colony, they use the sun as their compass. If it is cloudy or the sun has moved, they use a time correction factor to account for the sun's movement. In addition, honeybees are able to detect polarized light that penetrates clouds, acting as a backup navigational system to help track the sun. On a night of a full moon, workers continue to dance after dark – somehow compensating for the movement of the sun after sundown.

The fact that bees possess a memory for time

is intriguing. Von Frisch was able to train bees to arrive at feeding stations in three, four and five separate periods within 24 hours. Recent work by A.R. Smith and others at the Smithsonian Tropical Research Institute in Panama showed that social bees have a bigger brain area for both learning and memory compared to solitary bees. And like humans, bees show the effects of aging: David Münch and his team found that honeybees' memories fade and their ability to learn decreases. One way we both can slow down aging is by getting sleep: Barrett Klein and his coauthors found that sleep deprivation impairs the effectiveness of honeybees' waggle-dance signalling for communicating the location of food to their hive mates.

The fourth dance is the *vibrational* dance, where a worker vibrates her abdomen while holding the queen or a co-worker. This dance indicates either foraging or swarming activities. Pollen foragers use the vibrational dance to speed up other workers or convey information about daily and seasonal food availability, such as peaks. The vibrational dance can also alert the queen that nurse bees have begun to raise new queens. A few hours before swarming, the vibrational dance ceases throughout the entire colony. Once the swarm has departed, the remaining workers begin the vibrational dance once again – increasing the intensity after the first new queen has emerged.

The other dances von Frisch elaborated on include *jostling, spasmodic, buzzing run, shaking* and *trembling.* During the jostling dance, successful foragers return to the hive and jostle their co-workers by running and pushing them toward the "dance floor." The spasmodic dance functions to distribute food, but interspersed brief waggles signal a pending new-resource dance. The buzzing run denotes swarming. A shaking dance, which takes place from side to side, is a request from a co-worker for assistance in grooming. Finally, the exact function of the series of twitches, trembles and running on four legs called the trembling dance is unknown.

Researchers continue to explore the meanings and functions of these extraordinary dances of honeybees. Investigating how cocaine use exaggerates the dances of a forager bee has led a University of Illinois research team to suggest that there is a reward system in bees' brains. Other research focuses on the differences in dances between comparative samples of honeybee populations with more or less stress, such as habitat destruction or pesticide exposure. While the magnificent dances of honeybees communicate information to each other, humans can watch, listen and learn from their messages as well.

The Gifts They Give Us

The energy that honeybees invest into communication, foraging, production and reproduction also provides humans with many benefits.
There are several notable examples throughout
history that illustrate the timeless generosity of
bees. From energy-rich, medicinally beneficial
honey to beeswax, humans continually reap the
benefits of honeybees' hard work. Yet, as we will
see, the giving does not end there.

Honey

Open a "pot of gold(en)" honey and some of
the first osmophores, or scent molecules, reflect
petals of the nectar-providing flowers. The
colour, scent and taste of honey differ depending
on the local environment. Some, like California
heather or Oregon buckwheat, are dark, while
others such as Quebec's dandelion honey are

straw-coloured. From the Ohi'a tree's creamy Hawaiian Lehua to the water-like British Columbian or Alaskan fireweed, each honey has its own character. Australia's wonderfully spicy leatherwood honey stands in total contrast with the herbal-tasting eucalyptus. My favourite honey – and the title of a melodious 1971 song by Van Morrison – is tupelo honey. Its heavenly burnt-sugar tang comes from the tupelo trees in the swamps of Georgia and Florida.

Over 1.2 billion kilograms (2.65 billion pounds) of honey are produced each year. Honey contains over 200 substances. Bees secrete a glucose oxidase enzyme that assists in converting nectar into honey. Along with oxygen, the glucose enzyme splits the glucose molecule into water and hydrogen peroxide. Due to its hydrogen peroxide and glucose oxidase content, honey is a powerful antiseptic. High amounts of malic, citric, tartaric, oxalic and other organic acids combined with the enzymes catalase and peroxidase give honey its renowned antibacterial properties.

The ancient Mayans revered the stingless honeybees, and a thousand-year-old document of theirs, the Madrid Codex, pictures shamans successfully treating cataracts, conjunctivitis, chills and fever with honey-based medicines. With over 80 per cent sugar content and its natural acidity, honey creates an inhospitable environment for the single-celled microbes that form infections. The low water content of honey keeps bacteria, which thrive in water, from flourishing. Ancient Greeks and Romans had also discovered these properties of honey; they used honey to treat cataracts and heal open wounds. Some modern bandage companies line their products with diluted traces of honey.

Honey – in conjunction with wax – is also effective as an embalming fluid. Ancient Egyptians, Persians, Babylonians, Assyrians and Arabs preserved their important dead in this way. Even the ancient Greek king Alexander the Great – who died on foreign soil – is said to have arrived back home in Macedonia immersed in a honey-filled coffin. The preservative power of honey also works to its own advantage, as demonstrated by the sealed jars recovered from Egyptians' royal tombs that were found unspoiled, after thousands of years.

Honey is loaded with vitamins and minerals. It contains water-soluble B1, B2, B6, pantothenic and nicotinic acids, vitamin C – as well as high amounts of fat-soluble vitamins E, K and A. Honey also provides us with essential minerals: calcium, phosphorus, potassium, iron, copper, manganese, magnesium and sulfur. Some of these minerals in the specific concentrations found in honey mimic the concentration of blood serum. Thus, honey metabolizes easily and can be an important source of essential nutrients. In addition, the combination of glucose and fructose (monosaccharides) and some maltose, melezitose and dextrin makes honey an excellent source of caloric energy.

Some researchers suggest that a teaspoon or two of honey before bed ensures a restorative sleep. A human liver stores about eight hours of glycogen – an important brain food. If you eat supper at 7 pm, by about 3 am your brain releases a stress hormone called cortisol. Cortisol scavenges the body, melts muscle tissue and converts it into glycogen to feed the brain. When released, cortisol causes the heart to beat faster and raises glucose insulin levels in the blood.

Elevated cortisol can lead to obesity, diabetes, coronary disease and autoimmune breakdown. A teaspoon of honey at night fuels the liver with glucose and fructose, which is absorbed slowly – thus providing a restful sleep and preventing the release of cortisol. Honey's low glycemic index enables diabetics to also enjoy the reputed sleep benefits. Particularly, Floridian tupelo and New Zealand manuka honeys are best for diabetics. Children over the age of 2 can also benefit from honey, as it promotes learning and stimulates the area of developing tissue at the end of the long bones, called growth plates.

Importantly, we must be cautious when deciding which honey to purchase. In 2002, China, supplying the US with almost a third of its honey, shipped 70,000 kilograms (154,000 pounds) of honey contaminated with chloroamphenicol. The compound is banned in Australia, Canada, Europe, New Zealand and the United States, because although it treats anthrax, it also causes bone marrow failure through aplastic anemia. The Sara Lee Corporation, unknowingly, bought that contaminated honey and marketed a half million loaves of bread containing it. The next year, China finally banned chloroamphenicol.

The US annual honey consumption of over 180 million kilograms far outstrips the country's domestic supply. In fact, 2010 marked a record low honey production, dropping by over 9 million kilograms, or 12 per cent, to 65 million kilograms. China is the largest honey producer on the globe, but Chinese honey faces a stiff tariff when imported into the US. A group of executives at the German food-ingredient conglomerate Alfred L. Wolff GmbH, along with five other companies, allegedly conspired to illegally import $40-million worth of Chinese honey into the US and avoid $80-million in anti-dumping duties by labelling the product as originating from Malaysia, Indonesia, Taiwan and the Philippines. Some 2,400 drums of Chinese honey seized by US customs officers from storage facilities in Minnesota, Illinois and Washington State allegedly was also adulterated with antibiotics, in the largest food scandal so far recorded.

We cannot know how many other banned, toxic and carcinogenic chemicals are in use, so always ensure that the honey you purchase carries a recognized organic certified seal or consider supporting your local beekeeper by purchasing their honey.

Interestingly, there's a movement afoot all around the globe, from London to New York and Los Angeles to Melbourne, encouraging urban beekeepers to provide bees, assisting in pollinating our trees, plants and urban vegetable gardens in addition to harvesting safe sources of honey for their family and friends and occasionally for sale. Urban beekeeping has some very deep roots in the past: the archaeological work at the 3,000-year-old Tel Rehov townsite in Israel revealed about 200 hives that would have held about two million bees.

Honey hunters then and still

Modern appreciation of honey follows on the heels of an intriguing history. Early humans may have first discovered honey by observing other animals pursue the sweet riches. Chimpanzees in Africa, for instance, insert a stick or their hand into the bees' hive and remove it dripping with honey. The apes also use tools to break away wood around the flight hole in order to extract parts of the honeycomb. A number of other animals, including bears, skunks, foxes and honey buzzards, relish the energy-rich honey from the hives of bees.

One of the most intriguing honey-seeking partnerships is that of the African honeyguide bird and the ratel, or honey badger. The honeyguide has an unmistakable chirp that guides the ratel to a hive. The badger has strong legs, a thick hide that is impenetrable by bee stings, and paws specifically designed to rip apart honeybee nests. Once the badger has eaten its share of the honey and comb, the honeyguide moves in and eats the beeswax. Co-attackers, such as ants and small mammals, then consume any leftover larvae and honey.

To defend their territory, honeybees use potent stingers. The stingless honeybees of Central and South America, Australia and Indonesia defend their hives by attacking intruders' eyes, nose and ears. Some species even developed a mechanism for squirting a caustic fluid toward their attacker. Early honey hunters learned to carry smouldering vegetation to drive bees away and pacify them, allowing hunters to successfully loot honey caches.

A successful raid could result in a bounty of wax, propolis (bee glue), bee larvae (which provides a small amount of animal protein) and up to 45 kilograms (99 pounds) of honey.

Honey hunting may date back millions of years, into the Paleolithic period (Old Stone Age), but certainly took place during the Mesolithic period (Middle Stone Age). Depicted on cave walls around the world, the hunt for honey was – and still is – an important facet of many peoples and cultures.

Among other functions, caves offered these nomadic hunters and gatherers a space to communicate and keep records through drawings carved into the rock walls, called petroglyphs. Archeologists have documented almost 400 sites in 17 regions, including Europe, North and South Africa, India, Malaysia, Indonesia and Australia, where ancient peoples recorded the cherished honey hunt in detailed petroglyphs.

There is an incredible mysticism about this art. Some of the pictorial histories illustrate an aggressive hunt, while others show the bees almost *allowing* the extraction of their wares by these intrepid honey hunters. Rituals associated with the honey hunt often seem mysterious and spiritual. Researchers hypothesize that some hunters were actually clan shamans, reputed to have supernatural powers.

The first paintings of Mesolithic honey hunters to be discovered – in the 1920s – were the petroglyphs in the Cave of Spiders in Valencia, Spain. In the primary illustration, two figures are perched precariously on a vine ladder. The figure at the top – a collection basket tied to his waist – is raiding a hive. Over-large bees surround the hunter. The figure halfway up the ladder looks to be in awe, gazing up at the hunter.

Drawn around the same time as the Cave of Spiders images, the petroglyphs at Barranc Fondo in eastern Spain are far richer in detail. One image shows 11 detailed figures, including animals, standing at the base of a tree awaiting five honey hunters who are on a large ladder. Mystical creatures are hovering near the hive while swarms of bees attack the honey hunters. Two hunters are falling off the ladder, perhaps in agony from bee stings.

In central India too there is mesmerizing and colourful cave art that vividly documents how central the ritual of honey hunting was. The intricate details may actually have been a form of visualization, thus ensuring a triumphant hunt. The giant honeybees of India (*Apis dorsata*) are gregarious nesters, with some trees supporting over 200 colonies.

On the African continent there are more honey-hunting petroglyphs than anywhere else in the world. The Drakensberg Mountains of South Africa have over 40,000 paintings in 500 caves, spanning 3,000 years.

The direct descendants of those ancient honey hunters are the San peoples of present-day South Africa. Their spiritual nighttime ritual – as it was for their ancestors as well – is to dance for hours at the base of the hive tree, hypnotically humming into a deep trance. The hum of the San peoples is very similar to the vibrational thrum of the honeybees, perhaps enabling the San to calm the soon to be raided hives.

Another significant honey-hunting African people are the pygmies, currently numbering about 150,000. Their relatively small average height of 1.5 metres (4 feet 11 inches) allows manoeuvrability that works to their advantage during honey hunting. The Central African Aka pygmies hunt both honeybees and stingless honeybees for two months each year. Parties of five, including children, search the forest floor for ant nests near trees. Bees naturally die and fall to the foot of hive trees. Ants then carry off their bodies, dismember them in their nests and discard the inedible exoskeletons. Pygmy search parties look for these small middens glimmering in shafts of sunlight just outside the ants' entrance holes.

Once they identify a hive tree, the pygmies scan the trunk for an entrance hole. The honey hunter, an axe on his back and charcoal smeared on his face to protect himself from the forthcoming stings, uses lengths of vine to climb the tree. Tied to his waist is another length of vine which he uses to haul up smouldering wood wrapped in wet leaves.

As the hunter approaches the nest, he blows smoke into the hole to help calm the bees still in the hive. Many furious bees quickly exit to defend their territory by repeatedly stinging his mostly bare body. The hunter taps the bark to skilfully determine the exact location of the hive. Bracing himself against the trunk, with the vines for support, he chips away at the trunk with his axe.

Once the hole is large enough, the hunter reaches inside the hive and faces a second wave of infuriated bees. Somehow managing to disregard the painful stings, he carefully breaks off pieces of honeycomb and drops them to the forest floor, where the children quickly collect them. The party celebrates at the base of the tree by devouring some honeycomb, but ultimately the bulk of the treasure is divided among all of the pygmy families back at the village.

Similarly in Australia, Aborigines have, for thousands of years, hunted stingless honeybees (*Trigona* and *Austroplebia*, which they call "sugarbug") for their honey and propolis. Honey is, to this day, the backbone of Aborigines' diet and a mainstay in many of their rituals. Medicinally, they treat burns, lung ailments, eye infections, vomiting and diarrhea with honey.

Aboriginal honey hunters of northern Australia use their acute senses to locate trees that have hives within their trunks' hollow sections. Hunters search for a type of small, black lizard that lives near honey trees. These lizards pluck bees out of the air with their sticky tongues just before the bees enter the tree opening to their hive. Once the hive is located, the hunters chop notches into the trunk as footholds. Knocking on the bark with the back of their axes, they accurately determine, by the sound, the hive's location inside the tree cavity. They carve an opening to extract honeycomb and propolis. Once finished looting, the hunters repair the opening with mud so they can return in future months to the same hive.

Beeswax

Beeswax is a somewhat silent partner in the daily lives of people around the world. Each year, we use 20 million kilograms (44 million pounds) of beeswax – valued at $25-million. In fact, in 2007 Clorox paid almost a billion dollars for Burt's Bees, the specialty beeswax-based personal-care products company. From cosmetics, stick colognes, antiperspirants, candies and dental impressions to the mouthpieces of didgeridoos, beeswax is often an important component. Your pool table has beeswax filling its screw holes and the seams between the slates. Beeswax thread is still preferred by shoemakers – and sailors – because of its durability and incredible resistance to weathering. Furniture and automobile polish, industrial lubricants, paint removers and even the frets on a two-stringed Philippine kutiyapi boat-lute – they all rely on the wax of the bees.

Made of fatty acids and hydrocarbons, beeswax melts at a low temperature of 66°C (151°F). The Roman Catholic Church uses about 1.4 million kilograms (3.1 million pounds) of beeswax in their candles each year, which are 49 per cent beeswax.

In Asia, many textiles are hand-painted using a technique called batik, or wax-resist. In the batik process, covering sections of a pattern with beeswax allows those sections to resist any dye that is later applied. The same batik method creates the intricate designs on pysanky – Ukrainian Easter eggs. Since the lightest-colour dye is applied first, beeswax (often mixed with some paraffin for a cracking effect on textiles) is applied to the areas intended to be that light colour. Once dry, the wax resists any subsequent darker-coloured dyes. At the end of the process, the designer melts the beeswax off to reveal the whole pattern. Indonesia, India, Malaysia and

Thailand use the batik process, providing clothes for more than 1.5 billion people.

Unfortunately, beeswax is a sponge for toxic chemicals. Beehives exposed to CheckMite – a commercial pesticide used to kill *varroa*, a mite that is fatal to bees – results in beeswax contaminated with a carcinogenic organophosphate called coumaphos. Coumaphos is easily absorbed through the skin. Individuals exposed to this chemical experience a range of symptoms, including diminished lifespan, depending on the amount of exposure. This chemical infiltration into the bees' hive highlights the need to move beyond pesticides, herbicides, fungicides and miticides and toward a healthier future for both humans and bees.

Beyond the hive and into the future

As though the products of the beehive were not enough, humans are actively investigating even more ways to enrol bees to improve our well-being. Recent studies indicate, for example, that bees can count to four. With training, they appear to be able to count and return to a specific destination. While applications for their savvy number skills are as yet untapped, many of their other distinct qualities – such as sight, smell and venom – are proving quite useful. For instance, research on bees' complete-picture eyesight has yielded results that may enable advances in miniaturized optics technology.

Bees' 170 smell receptors and nearly perfect accuracy in locating smells hold potential as a diagnostic tool. Nobel laureate Ivan Pavlov's classic work on conditioned reflexes has been harnessed to teach bees to respond to more than 60 odours, from methamphetamine to TNT and from enriched uranium to tuberculosis. In order to get the bees to identify a scent, the chemicals are mixed into a sugary liquid laced with a hit of caffeine, which the bees are rewarded with. The process is repeated up to five times, by which point the bees associate the smell with the food. Thereafter, when a bee encounters a desirable scent, its reflexes cause it to extend its proboscis, or tongue, to lap up the nectar – a reflex that scientists are easily able to measure.

Inevitably, this work has caught the attention of the security industry. Such applications would be particularly useful in the fight against terrorism – including bomb plots such as the one uncovered in 2010 that attempted to smuggle explosives in UPS courier shipments from Yemen. Soon, bees could be deployed in war zones, airports, train stations, ports, sports arenas, food service companies, the housing industry and medical offices. The economics certainly make sense. Sniffer dogs, which can cost about $9,000 each, are accurate about 71 per cent of the time and require at least three months' training. Honeybees are accurate 98 per cent of the time and require less than 10 minutes' training and thus would come at a fraction of the cost. Moreover, they can detect explosives or narcotics in the presence of potentially interfering agents such as lotions, motor oil or insect repellent. And after a couple days of sniffing duty, they can be returned, unharmed, to the hive.

Bees also outperform most technological solutions. Many airports have now installed full-body scanners, at a cost of $200,000 per device. Yet even if Abdul Farouk Abdulmutallab, the young Nigerian who in 2009 concealed explosives in his underpants in an attempt to blow up a passenger jet, had been full-body scanned, there would have been only a 50 to 60 per cent chance of detecting those explosives. With more than 85,000 commercial flights across the globe every day, those are unacceptable odds. A British company, Inscentinel Ltd., has developed an ingenious device that uses bees to sniff out narcotics, homemade fertilizer bombs, plastic explosives and 60 or so other dangerous substances. Three bees are placed inside a shoe-box-sized "sniffer box." Air is sucked in via tubes and wafted gently over the bees. If they detect explosives or narcotics they all stick out their tongues, sending an alarm to the operator.

There are also humanitarian uses for sniffer bees. The Red Cross estimates that between 50 million and 100 million landmines exist in 80 countries, maiming 22,000 people (mostly children) every year. A system devised by the University of Montana counters this by fitting honeybees with miniature microchips. As the bees fly around, the electrostatic charge on their bodies attracts TNT residue, the explosive component of landmines. Once they return to the hive, this can be detected, and a scan of the chip will reveal the location of the explosive.

These techniques could also be applied to the health system. Honeybees are already being used as early detectors of lung and skin cancers, diabetes and TB, as well as in monitoring fertility cycles and confirming pregnancies. Patients breathe into a glass diagnostic tool, and when the trained bees detect the smell of any of the diseases or hormones, they move toward the tubes that lead closer to the breath.

Since 1957, the former USSR has used extracts of bee stings – bee venom, known as apis – to treat rheumatoid arthritis, multiple sclerosis and other debilitating autoimmune diseases. Bee venom contains biochemicals that enhance blood flow to the damaged regions and block the perception of neuralgic pain. Currently dubbed apitherapy, apis treatment is on the rise throughout the world. Taking advantage of the anti-inflammatory effects of melittin and adolapin in bee venom – along with apamin to improve nerve transmission – apis can treat arthritis, fibromyalgia and tendonitis. In fact, 12 European countries have officially recognized bee venom solution as a drug.

Bees and Food Production

There are over 330 million mouths to feed in Canada and the United States alone. The honeybees are directly responsible for pollinating over $44-billion worth of food and commodities each year in both countries, including melons, gourds, pears, plums, peaches, kiwis, macadamias, sunflowers, canola, avocados, lettuce, broccoli and cotton. The beef and dairy industries rely on bees to pollinate the alfalfa and clover fields for feed. Even corporations such as Starbucks and General Mills – owner of Häagen-Dazs – rely on bees to pollinate their coffee and more than half of their ice cream ingredients.

Beekeepers are struggling to sustain themselves. With the wholesale price of honey hovering around us$3 per pound (2005–2009), they must rent out their colonies. About three million honeybee hives are used in food production in Canada and the US. In the US the scale and scope of the operation is mind boggling, given that many of the 2.4 million hives spend most of their time on trailers being trucked back and forth across the country.

Billions of bees travel great distances to pollinate entire harvests of almonds, apples, blueberries, cherries, cranberries, cucumbers, grapes and tomatoes, to name only a few more. For instance, a beekeeper may begin the season by having their bees pollinate citrus in Florida. They then may head north to do the blueberries and cranberries of Maine, then west to the Dakotas to pollinate clover and alfalfa. Perhaps a stop in Kansas or Missouri in the fall for goldenrod (which makes delicious honey) precedes their likely winter home in California to get ready for the enormous pollination effort on the almond plantations in early February.

Hives in Canada are not quite as nomadic. Alberta's beekeepers transport their hives into British Columbia to service the blueberry fields. New Brunswick's blueberries use hives from Nova Scotia and Quebec for pollination.

The cotton industry in the US alone generates $27-billion in revenue through various sectors, including clothing, and food in the form of cottonseed oil, shortening, salad dressing, crackers, cookies and chips. Grown in 17 states on over 18,600 farms, cotton covers 4.2 million hectares (10.4 million acres) of land in the US. Despite the massive assistance bees provide for growing these crops, the cotton industry uses 34 million kilograms (75 million pounds) of pesticides each year. According to the US Environmental Protection Agency (EPA), a dozen of these pesticides are carcinogenic.

Almonds, for example

High in fibre, rich in vitamin E and loaded with antioxidants that help prevent heart disease and cancers, almonds are now one of the favourite nut varieties. Originally from Asia, both the almond and its close cousin the peach evolved to thrive in North America. While the peach offers a delicious, fleshy fruit with a stone-seed pit, the almond bears a thick, fibrous hull encasing the prized edible seed – the nut. California's Sacramento and San Joaquin valleys grow 82 per cent of the world's almonds – over 682 million kilograms (1.5 billion pounds).

Almond flowers require bees as their pollinator. To attain a bumper crop, 100 per cent of the flowers require pollination, which is unlikely to happen in the wild. Growers must graft at least a couple of varieties in their plantations because nature requires cross-pollination between varieties of almonds, not within a single variety. Almond growers are able to force this massive monoculture plantation (322,000 hectares, or 796,000 acres) by densely loading onto their land about 550,000 honeybees per hectare (nearly a quarter-million bees per acre). Over 1.5 million healthy hives – 75 billion bees – must apply their Herculean efforts to realize this astounding 100 per cent pollination mark. And recently, Western Australia has entered into growing almonds, with 1.25 million saplings planted – now they too will conscript tens of millions of honeybees to produce the prized nuts.

In 2004, the almond growers were paying nearly $40 per hive. In 2006/07, after an enormous honeybee collapse, the price per hive soared to $150. As bee populations continue to diminish, the escalating prices large-scale agriculture will have to pay for bees' services has vast economic implications. Not only does this development increasingly affect our smaller-scale farmers and the market prices we pay at retail, it also bolsters the drive to turn bees into even more of a commodity. Those who breed genetically modified bees or own the bulk of bee populations stand to profit greatly. For the rest of us, however, that potential signals a precarious future.

Industrial agriculture: A call for change

Agriculture systems need to mimic the structure and function of indigenous ecosystems by working with the native plant communities. The grandfather of organic farming, Sir Albert Howard, understood that any agriculture system is only as good as its soil. Plant roots and soil are living, breathing, breeding communities of trillions of bacteria, fungi, protozoa, nematodes, micro-arthropods, worms, beetles and so much more. They decompose recently died plant materials and add them to the humus layer, ensuring the structure, aeration and water retention of the soil. Plant roots also actively release food into the soil to promote micro-organism development.

Modern agriculture systems use chemical pesticides, fumigants, fungicides, herbicides and fertilizers that kill a vast range of beneficial micro-organisms. Micro-organisms promote healthy plant growth, boost plant defence mechanisms and naturally break down pollutants in the soil. In fact, conventional agriculture has reduced bacterial numbers from trillions per gram of soil in the root zone to a mere couple of million.

Weakened plants are obviously more susceptible to disease and infestations. In turn, the plants' weakness serves to justify further dependence on chemical pesticides. Of course, this continues to weaken and destroy the extremely diverse web of life in soil biology. To compound the problem, in North America alone over 500 agricultural pests are now resistant to our latest pesticides.

The Soil Foodweb Institute has identified and quantified these problems over years of research by a variety of specialists. The Institute has developed an excellent, economically viable solution to naturally nourish and rejuvenate soil ecosystems. After assessing soils for their deficiencies, the Institute brews up a compost tea – a liquid produced by leaching soluble nutrients and extracting bacteria, fungi, protozoa and nematodes from compost. The tea inoculates microbial life into the soil or onto the foliage of the crop plants, adding necessary soluble nutrients for foliar and soil ecosystems. The process invigorates both micro-organisms and plant life.

Globally, humans rely on about 20 plant species for our staple food source. Maintaining the soil food web of life is the *only* way our planet will be able to feed the burgeoning human population, by allowing for truly sustainable agriculture in the 21st century.

For over 20 years, the Land Institute in Kansas has examined the ecology of the Great Plains Grassland and broadened understanding of nitrogen fixers, native plants, natural plant defence mechanisms and beneficial insects. Not surprisingly, these native communities work together to provide essential habitat for pollinators such as bumble and solitary bees, moths, bats and hummingbirds.

Nitrogen fixers are enriching members of the soil community. They are plants that take nitrogen gas from the air and, with the assistance of root bacterial nodules, add it into the soil. By using native nitrogen fixers in the field, there is no need for chemical-based nitrate fertilizers, which are inorganic salts that destroy the soil biology.

Native plants with both deep and shallow roots have adapted to different sources of moisture. Plant life on the Great Plains Grassland, including the renowned grasses, has figured out how to contend with aridity. The plants invest as much as 80 per cent of their growth into roots, promoting healthy soil biology. The Land Institute has documented over 230 native perennial plant species in Kansas that provide constant ground cover throughout the growing season and soak up every drop from convectional downpours. Of the more than 230 documented plants, there are between 20 and 30 nitrogen fixers – nature's way of fertilizing the soil food web.

In Kansas, modern agriculture's monoculture fields of wheat experience eight times as much runoff as the wild prairie does. Considering this fact, the Land Institute has developed a system called polyculture. Polyculture mixes native species of plants in plots similar to how they exist in nature.

The Institute has found four particular crops that produce significantly greater yields compared to the local monoculture crops. The first is Eastern gama grass (*Tripsacum dactyloides*), a cousin of corn that makes terrific meal. Secondly, a legume eaten by livestock called Illinois bundle flower (*Desmanthus illinoensis*). Third is mammoth wild rye (*Leymus racemosus*), a close cousin of wheat that the Mongols successfully used during droughts. Finally, Maximilian's sunflower (*Helianthus maximiliana*) is an oil-rich seed able to supply vegetable oil or biodiesel. Not only are all four plants biologically compatible, but when planted together their combined yield skyrockets. Compatible species in nature provide each other with biochemical protection and moisture, a knockout one-two punch combination.

There are numerous other forward-thinking agriculture systems springing up around the globe. All of these movements have a significant role to play in guiding us away from the toxic future currently facing us and toward a path of self-sufficiency. Looking back and learning from our – often forgotten – natural environments brings all life on our planet closer to a healthier existence. Some of the solutions are in our cities and even our own back yards. For instance, consider that a colony of bees requires the equivalent of 20 football fields, each full of flowers, to make a living for 30 days. In our urban green spaces or in the wild, about 40 full-sized maple, basswood, black locust, magnolia, eucalyptus, apple and tulip trees per half-hectare have roughly one million blossoms that can also support one colony of bees for part of their harvesting season. Urban trees are tremendous, not just for their capacity to help remove rising carbon dioxide from the atmosphere and replenish oxygen or to provide habitat for critters as well as shade on a hot summer afternoon, but importantly they offer safe nectar and pollen for all the wild bees.

In the meantime, there are at least two populations of honeybees in remote locations on Earth that remain disease-free and offer new genetic traits that could bolster our beleaguered bees against the toxic world we have inadvertently created. There are about three million honeybees in the least populous and most remote jurisdiction in the world, the Pitcairn Islands. These bees feast on mango, lata, passion fruit, guava and rose-apple flowers and produce a rich, intensely fruity honey that is exported around the world – if you ever get the opportunity, treat yourself to this exquisite honey; your taste buds will never forget it. The other isolated honeybees were recently found in the Sahara desert in southeastern Libya, which 10,000 years ago was lush savannah. They have remained isolated at the Kufra Oasis in an area of 88 square kilometres separated by more than 800 kilometres of sandy desert from cities on the Mediterranean. These wild honeybees are free of parasites, including the lethal *varroa* mites which have decimated colonies around the globe.

These two examples give us hope that the answers to diseases, not only of the bees but of all living things, can be found in wild ecosystems – our legacy to our children – and give further credence to the wisdom of protecting areas that have not been developed or spoiled by human beings.

Down a Path We Can't Sustain

Many ancient cultures revered bees for their honey, yet most had no idea of their overall global importance as partners in the plant kingdom. The Mayans are the notable exception. Almost 2,000 years ago, the Mayans very clearly understood that the health of the stingless bees was central to their very existence; they entrusted this protective role to their most sacred shaman.

One stingless beehive in Central America requires about 482 square kilometres (186 square miles) of jungle to fill its comb with honey. The health of the jungle also depends on bees cross-pollinating. Stingless bees in particular evolved to pollinate the vanilla orchid, which yields a lucrative vanilla pod used as a spice. Deforestation and widespread use of insecticides have destroyed the bees' habitat, resulting in the extinction of the stingless honeybee populations in Mexico and

Central America. Humans must now attempt to hand-pollinate these marvellous plants by peeling back a flap that is accessible for only one day a year.

Or consider springtime along the hillsides in the province of Sichuan, China. The pear trees transform an otherwise green landscape into a soft white, as a billion flowers grow. Well-documented carcinogens – organophosphate insecticides – are so prevalent that no beekeeper will venture into these plantations. The entire native bumble and solitary bee populations are dead from years of toxicity. In turn, thousands of migrant workers – including women and children – dangle from the pear tree limbs as they attempt to hand-pollinate each flower.

Yet, we do not have to look back in time or outside of our own backyard to discuss the devastation of ecosystems – including our beloved bees. In Europe, Canada and the United States, honeybee populations have plummeted dramatically over the past few years. In late 2006, beekeepers discovered – almost overnight – millions of nearly abandoned hives with no trace of any dead bodies. Colony Collapse Disorder (CCD) is the name of this widespread and ongoing condition. Hives suffering from CCD are loaded with brood (immature bees) and honeycomb, but only the queen and a few workers remain; all are very nervous and completely disoriented.

Bee populations are suffering throughout the world. In the UK over the past century, the number of beehives has reportedly declined by nearly 75 per cent, from over a million to 280,000. Since the 1930s the UK has lost 97 per cent of its wildflowers and the repercussions have been devastating on all pollinators, especially the bees, which halved in just the last 25 years. In the US, honeybee colonies declined by nearly 36 per cent over the winter of 2007 to 2008, 29 per cent from 2008 to 2009, 34 per cent from 2009 to 2010, and 30 per cent from 2010 to 2011, according to a study by the US Department of Agriculture. Despite increased awareness and research, 30 per cent is only a slight improvement from the previous four years. The decline in Canadian honeybee numbers over the past four years has ranged between 21 and 35 per cent. The one notable exception is the commercial beekeepers of Ontario, who recently reported a mortality rate of 43 per cent in 2010/11.

While the media desperately sought a "smoking gun," they lost sight of the marvellous complexity of biological systems. Scientists endeavour to discover and understand pieces of the rich tapestry of life. Yet, when applied science attempts to solve problems in ecosystems, it is very difficult to find a single cause and effect. It is always more likely that a number of factors – acting together – cause a breakdown. Thus, the answer to why billions of bees are disappearing worldwide is not one single smoking gun, but a whole arsenal.

Research into the causes of CCD is focusing on the following areas: pathogens and parasites, bee management stresses like poor nutrition, and environmental stresses such as pesticides. While there is no causal relationship established yet, we will briefly consider some of the armaments in the above research categories that may be working in concert to debilitate the bee populations.

The honeybees have one distinct advantage that emboldens hope for their plight. In 2006, their genome was fully decoded. Knowing the nearly ten thousand genes of the honeybee opens up vast potential for research into CCD and its related causes. For instance, the decoded genome reveals that honeybees have only half as many genes for detoxification and immunity as other insects. Interestingly, bees from around the globe have the same sets of "good" bacteria inside their stomachs and intestines. These specific bacteria are unique to bees and are of paramount importance for bees to fight pathogens and detoxify pesticides.

A University of Illinois research team recently (2009) compared the genome of healthy hives and hives suffering from CCD in two geographical regions. Particularly, they looked at the genes active in the stomachs and intestines and consistently found atypical fragments of ribosomal RNA in CCD-afflicted bees. Such damage to ribosomes impacts protein production and the health of the bee as a whole. With compromised ribosomes, the bee cannot produce the necessary proteins to effectively act against parasites, viruses, pesticides and other threats. Honeybees are currently suffering extremely high disease loads such as deformed-wing virus, Israeli acute paralysis virus, sacbrood virus, black queen cell virus, Kashmir bee virus and others – 14, to be exact. In general, higher viral loads are consistently present in colonies suffering from CCD. Whether this phenomenon is a potential cause or a potential effect of an already weakened immune system is a current topic of investigation.

A lot of attention has been given to the Israeli acute paralysis virus (IAPV), which causes bees to shiver until paralysis and death. Since 2002 in the US, the virus has mutated at least twice from its original Israeli form. Both Canada and the US import hundreds of thousands of honeybees from Australia, and when the Israeli virus was found on some Australian honeybees in 2006/07 it was – again – incorrectly fingered as the single cause of CCD. Current research suggests that IAPV is still considered one of the factors involved in CCD. In 2010, 11 species of wild pollinators, including bumble bees, have turned up carrying some of the viruses known to plague domestic honeybees, believed to be picked up from shared flower pollen. IAPV showed up in wild pollinators near honeybee installations carrying the disease. This raises concerns about possible virus transmission through the 200 tons of honeybee-collected pollen used to feed bumble bees in bee-raising operations worldwide.

Introduction of other diseases from captive-bred bumble bees used for pollination of greenhouse crops into wild bumble bee populations is also believed to be a worldwide threat to our wild bees. In the UK, for instance, three of the 25 British species of bumble bees are already extinct and half of the remainder have shown serious declines, often up to 70 per cent, since around 1970. British scientists with the Insect Pollinator Initiative are examining the crash of the remaining populations. In the meantime this is a wake-up call that the bumble bee species are declining, not only in Europe, not only in Asia, but in North America as well.

Varroa destructor is a voracious microscopic mite that originated in Asia. After attacking the Asian honeybee (*Apis cerana*), the mites jumped cargo ships and hitchhiked to Florida, arriving in 1987. Since then, they have wreaked havoc throughout North America (and elsewhere), killing millions of honeybee colonies. Tracheal and *varroa* mites cause immuno-suppression in bees by secreting a substance that prevents the bees from producing the enzymes and antimicrobial peptides that usually fend off invasion. Recent research suggests that this carrier of picorna-like viruses may initiate ribosome breakdown. Attempts to provide protection with a number of fluvalinate pesticides, including Apistan and CheckMite – recall that this chemical also contaminates beeswax – have only resulted in the mites developing resistance. So far, only Hawaii and Australia are free of these destructive mites.

The Italian honeybee was introduced into Australia repeatedly in the 19th century, and up until very recently it posed no noticeable threat to the well-being of that country's honeybee populations. As a result, Australia has been exporting healthy queens around the globe. In 2007, however, a vessel arrived in Cairns, northern Queensland, with a colony of Asian honeybees in its mast. Not only are Asian honeybees poor honey producers, but they also rob other hives. They've been spreading at the rate of about 100 kilometres (62 miles) a year, and though the government had been conducting an aggressive Asian honeybee eradication program, in March 2011 the program was cancelled. According to a bee pathologist with Australia's national science agency, the Commonwealth

Scientific & Industrial Research Organization, the Asian honeybee will spread throughout most of Australia, very likely jeopardizing the health of Australia's honeybees and ultimately curtailing the export of queens.

Another parasite attacking bees is *Nosema ceranae* – a parasitic fungus that first afflicted the Asian honeybee. Discovered in the early 1990s in North America and in 2003 in Europe, the fungus was also once falsely accused as the sole cause of CCD. *Nosema* infiltrates a bee's intestines, where the fungus nuclei divide repeatedly and produce organisms. A DNA-based virus is linked to the fungus, which proliferates in cool, damp weather and thrives in the bees' gut, disrupting their nutrition and eventually destroying their digestive system. The antibiotic fumagillin is the regular treatment for hives infected with this fungus, a treatment that is also linked to the dramatic increase in disease loads, as it weakens the bees' immune systems.

In North America and elsewhere, our captive honeybees are being overworked and undernourished. In the US, honeybees are exposed to toxic endocrine-disrupting chemicals and fed high-fructose corn syrup and monoculture pollen. Beekeepers around the globe are attempting to combat this management stress on bees by changing the food they provide for their hives. One example of this is a form of protein shake that consists of eggs, brewer's yeast, pollen, honey and other special ingredients.

Poor nutrition is also impacting non-captive bees through a combination of environmental stresses. Air pollution, for example, is interfering with the ability of bees to find flowering plants, because scents that could travel more than 800 metres in the 1800s now reach less than 200 metres from a plant. In addition, the abnormally high temperatures of 2006 were quite likely the tipping point for the bees in North America. The searingly hot springtime, right during the onset of flowering, may have caused sterile pollen in many plants. In 2007, tests of almond, plum, kiwi and cherry pollen revealed little, if any, protein content. Infertile soils lacking essential nutrients, bacteria, fungi and protozoa – along with global warming – worked together to cause this phenomenon.

Global warming is having a profound impact

on weather patterns, reducing the snowfall in the southern Rockies, which supplies meltwater to the Colorado River and 25 million people in the southwestern US as well as Mexico. Snowpacks are melting three weeks earlier, causing glacier lilies to emerge at least a couple of weeks sooner. A climate-driven mismatch is now occurring, as the bumble bees that pollinate the lilies are waking up two weeks too late. The fate of the lilies is in jeopardy. It's happening around the nation. In Maryland, honeybees, which rely heavily on the first bloom to generate copious amounts of honey to sustain their hives for the year, are having to quickly change their diets because plants are flowering as much as four weeks earlier. This change is evident from Maryland honey, which traditionally was a rich, red colour with an earthy flavour from the American tulip trees. Now the bees are producing a fruitier honey, as they are relying on later-blooming black locust trees to make a living. The changes in both the Rockies and Maryland have happened fast, within two decades. The trees, bees and other critters are unequivocally telling scientists that the Earth is warming up.

Before we wade into the environmental stress caused by pesticides, it is worth mentioning the debilitating effect of electromagnetic radiation on bees. Cellular phone towers emit high frequencies of radiation as they provide coverage across landmasses. Although cell phones and towers are not, thankfully, found in high concentrations in farmers' fields or wild forests and meadows, recent studies have shown some disturbing results that impair bees foraging near towns or cities around the globe. A cellular phone placed immediately next to a beehive and emitting a frequency of 900 MHz in 10-minute bursts over a short period of 10 days caused honey production to cease during each 10-minute interval. The queens in the test colonies produced significantly fewer eggs per day (100) compared to the queens unexposed to cellular radiation (350 eggs per day). When a cellular phone call is made or received honeybees react by making a "piping" noise, which is a precursor of either swarming or a disturbed colony. The piping noise increases tenfold each time a cellular call is activated. The high-frequency radiation emitted by a cellular phone clearly disrupts the magnetite crystals in the bees' fat-body cells, which present magnetic remanence. These magnetite structures are an essential part of the magnetoreception systems in honeybees. Cellular radiation is harmful to bees and its deleterious effects are being further studied.

Pesticides and the damage done

Each year, our global biosphere endures an onslaught of some 2.3 billion kilograms (5 billion pounds) of pesticides. Many of these pesticides are neonicotinoids, which synthetically mimic a plant compound found in tomatoes, potatoes, peppers and tobacco. A neuro-active insecticide fashioned after nicotine, neonicotinoids poison nerves and prevent acetylcholine from enabling neurons to communicate with each other and with muscle tissue. In humans, for instance, these substances would trigger Parkinson's and Alzheimer's diseases.

A subsidiary of the pharmaceutical company Bayer (the Aspirin people), called Bayer CropScience, manufactures the pesticides clothianidin (called Poncho in Europe) and imidacloprid (called Gaucho in France). They are forms of neonicotinoid. In France in 1999, a third of the honeybee population died due to the use of Gaucho, an effect which the French referred to as "mad bee disease." Over the next five years, authorities progressively banned its use on selected crops, and in 2008 Gaucho was banned altogether. In 2008 Germany too banned eight neonicotinoid seed-treatment products, including Poncho, because of the devastating impact they have on bee populations.

Bayer representatives claim that application errors were to blame for the chemicals ending up in the air and affecting bees. That said, warning labels on these pesticides indicate the following – familiar – post-exposure symptoms: memory loss, appetite loss, disorientation and immune system collapse. Despite all the controversy and evidence, these products are still widely used throughout North America. In December 2010 a leaked EPA document revealed that Bayer had incorrectly tested clothianidin in a flawed scientific study which enabled them to register the neonicotinoids in 2003. Germany, France, Italy and Slovenia have banned clothianidin for its known toxic effects, and finally it's being scrutinized in the US.

Dutch toxicologist Dr. Henk Tennekes's latest book, *The Systemic Insecticides: A Disaster in the Making*, concisely documented that neonicotinoids are water soluble, mobile in soils and persistent for decades in both soil and water. Imidacloprid contaminated western Dutch surface waters and killed springtails, beetles and earthworms, robbing the soil of its necessary beneficial fauna, which decompose leaf litter and other organic matter and recycle nutrients. Those insects, in turn, are a crucial food source for many common grassland bird species. Moving up the food chain, Tennekes discovered that populations of avian predators like eurasian goshawks and northern goshawks have likewise fallen, dramatically. The use of these potent neonicotinoids has exhibited a deleterious effect on biodiversity and the web of life throughout western Europe.

In Canada, beekeepers in New Brunswick, Prince Edward Island and Vancouver Island have experienced serious declines in their bee populations – between 50 and 90 per cent colony loss since 1999. These beekeepers believe that imidacloprid – under the trade name Admire – is responsible. The chemical residues collect in the pollen and nectar of crops pollinated by honeybees. In turn, bees repeatedly ingest the chemicals and slowly die. Similar concerns have been raised in Ontario potato-farming areas.

As early as 2005, scientists were alarmed by the amounts of pesticides that were turning up in hives. One study found 66 different pesticides in one hive. Not only were three-quarters of these insecticides toxic to bees, their combined effect multiplied the toxicity by over 900 times. In March of 2010, research conducted in 23 US states and three Canadian provinces found 121 different pesticides in 887 samples of bees, wax, pollen and hives. Levels of toxicity are so high now that honeybees are detecting that pollen in the hive is tainted with pesticides because it lacks the microbial activity that characterizes pollen that has less pesticide residue. Honeybees are entombing or sealing up hive cells with toxic pollen. It's a last-ditch effort to save themselves but it appears to be unsuccessful, as the presence of encapsulated pollen cells is a predictor of colony loss.

In 2008, researchers from Penn State University found evidence of 43 different pesticide varieties in Pennsylvania apple orchards. Some farmers "stack" chemicals – that is, mix them together in a single broadcast application. The US EPA has no data on stacking. They rely on Bayer, BASF, Dow, Monsanto, DuPont and Syngenta to do all the safety tests. The EPA does not conduct independent tests of herbicides, pesticides, fungicides and miticides unless a worthy calamity occurs.

Even more disturbing are results from mixing a neonicotinoid with the fungicide Procure. Procure combats powdery mildew on melons, squash, pumpkins, cucumbers, zucchini, apples, pears, strawberries and cherries – all pollinated plants. Mixing increases toxicity to honeybees more than a thousandfold. The gross overuse of herbicides, pesticides, fungicides and miticides – individually and stacked – drastically weakens bees' autoimmune systems.

The present agriculture system uses so much pesticide that if the stuff were packed in 45-kilogram (99-pound) sacks, it would encircle the entire planet. Clearly, industrial-scale agriculture desperately needs restructuring. When that deleterious system combines with climate change and a beleaguered worldwide bee population, we know this is not the best way forward. Today more than ever, we need to respect nature and interpret her warning signposts – such as billions of dying bees. Change is opportunity in disguise. By aiming to work within nature's blueprint, our species has a golden opportunity to flourish in the 21st century.

How To Help the Bees Recover

Businesses involved with agriculture – directly or indirectly – are responsible for forcing the most stress on our ecosystems, but they also have the resources to improve the situation. While we actively wait for them to realize the benefits of answering calls for change, it is at the local level that each of us has the power to act. In various segments of society there are movements to protect our environment. There are many ways to take action and participate in making our world a healthier place – for bees, humans and life as a whole.

Conservation biology, for instance, is a relatively new branch in science; its mandate is to protect the genetic tapestry of life on Earth. Life on land and under the sea holds the cure for every disease. In fact, an entire new industry with legions of engineers and scientists has cropped up, called biomimicry. Biomimicry uses nature's own innovations to solve engineering, materials science and medical problems. While not all of us are scientists, this need not stop us from tapping into the incredibly important research that is happening all around us. From a quick Google search for information to getting involved with projects in your area, you too can participate by increasing your understanding of the issues.

Recently, US First Lady Michelle Obama created an organic garden on the White House lawn. Right next to it are two honeybee hives with an official "keeper." New surges of urban beekeepers are making headlines around the world. Yet, we do not have to keep bees in order to nurture and protect them. There are actions to take in multiple areas of our lives that will help to respect – and give back to – the incomparable honeybees that give so much to us. After all, we are inextricably linked in this dance of planetary survival.

Since the UK has lost more than 3 million hectares (7.4 million acres) of wildflowers since the Second World War The Co-operative supermarket chain is recreating wildflowers and nectar-rich plants like lesser knapweed, field scabious and birdsfoot trefoil. Wildflowers are being planted along roadsides, fields and houses to create a network of green corridors, or "bee roads," where insects can feed and move around the country more easily. Farmers and other landowners are sowing wildflowers in two long rows, which will stretch north to south and east to west across Yorkshire, restoring a total of five hectares (12 acres) of land as of spring 2011 in a pilot project. And the employees of Rowse Honey raised £100,000 (us$160,000) for the British Beekeepers Association with a series of clever television advertisements involving the public by asking them to vote for their favourite commercial.

It is not unimaginable that the honeybees could be yet another vital resource that gets commodified eventually. Imagine having to order and pay to have bees brought to your garden to pollinate. Or what would the price of food be once only a handful of corporations hold the "patent" or "licence" for all remaining (or genetically modified) honeybees? While these ideas may seem extreme, we need only look to the decade-long litigation between agribusiness giant Monsanto and Saskatchewan farmers Percy and Louise Schmeiser. This farm couple's legal battle illustrates how the corporations responsible for vigorously promoting modified crops and the use of chemicals could end up ultimately profiting from the eventual total decline of the species they quietly help to destroy.

In the end, consider all you have learned about the bees – their history and current status. While they continually give to us, we humans have regrettably neglected our dynamic little friends. Here is a list of ways you can help the bees. Let's hope that next year's reports show bee populations increasing from their currently depleted numbers.

Things a person can do:

○ Buy organic foods.
○ Buy organic cotton.
○ Support your local beekeepers by purchasing organic honey.
○ Do not use herbicides, pesticides, fungicides or miticides in your yard. When insecticides

are necessary, the Indian neem tree is a wonderful natural powerhouse. Neem-based products do not harm bees, moths, bats, hummingbirds or any other beneficial insect such as spiders, ladybugs, dragonflies. Neem products don't harm any warm-blooded animals or birds either.

○ Plant a wide variety of native flowers – especially yellows and blues in solid blocks of 1 × 1 metres (3 × 3 feet) so that bees can see them.

○ Provide somewhere for bees to live in your yard, such as dead tree branches, old animal burrows or wooden bee blocks.

○ Visit the website of the USDA Agriculture Research Service Logan Bee Lab for details on bee-friendly wild flowers: www.ars.usda .gov/Services/docs.htm?docid=12052.

○ To find out how to build a pollinator garden, visit www.pollinator.org.

○ Let some of your garden's leafy plants go to seed at the end of the season; they'll provide food for some species of bees before the colder months.

○ Bees need water, too, so place a bowl with water in your yard and replenish it regularly.

○ If in Illinois, join Bee Spotter and help scientists learn what species are in your area: http://beespotter.mste.uiuc.edu. If not in Illinois, check out the Bee Spotter site and consider starting one for your own area.

Global warming has dramatically affected plants by speeding up the timing of flowering. Native bees and other pollinators time their awakening in the spring with floral blooms. If pollinators time their spring emergence incorrectly and miss the bloom, both plants and animals perish. Thousands of volunteers are helping plant scientists and beekeepers track the timing of local blooms.

○ In Canada, consider participating in one of the "watch" programs through Nature Watch: www.icewatch.ca/english.
For specific provinces, find the plant watch organizations that you can "get involved" with – such as, in Alberta, at http://plant watch.fanweb.ca/.
○ If in the US, consider participating in the National Phenology Network: www .usanpn.org.

- Support organizations that protect wildland habitat, e.g., Nature Conservancy, Ducks Unlimited, Conservation International, The Land Conservancy or other, local agencies.
- Visit the From the Soil Up website and get tips on working with natural systems: www.fromthesoilup.com.au.
- Support the increase in grazing cows by purchasing free-range beef. Grazing cows do not require (much, if any) Tylosin or other antibiotics, and vacant fields are crucial habitat for bumble and solitary bees.
- Consider supporting organizations such as Bees without Borders www.beeswithoutborders.org/.

There is a worldwide movement afoot to follow nature's blueprint. Get curious and get involved!

Bookshelf

Airzee, S., et al. (pupils of Blackawton Primary School, Devon, UK). "Blackawton bees." *Biology Letters 7*, no. 2 (April 23, 2011): 168–172. Full text available at http://is.gd/bcmvnZ (accessed June 20, 2011).

Benjamin, Allison, and Brian McCallum. *A World without Bees*. London: Pegasus Books, 2009.

Bishop, Holley. *Robbing the Bees: A Biography of Honey, The Sweet Liquid Gold that Seduced the World*. New York: Free Press, 2005.

Buchmann, Stephen, and Banning Repplier. *Letters from the Hive: An Intimate History of Bees, Honey, and Humankind*. New York: Bantam, 2005.

Crane, Eva. *The World History of Beekeeping and Honey Hunting*. London: Duckworth, 2000.

Crane, Eva, and Harold Pager. *The Rock Art of Honey Hunters*. Cardiff: International Bee Research Association, 2001.

Favre, Daniel. "Mobile-phone-induced honeybee worker piping." *Apidologie, Online First* (April 13, 2011). Full-text available at http://is.gd/bFVgN6 (accessed June 30, 2011).

Halter, Reese. *Wild Weather*. Canmore, Alta.: Altitude Publishers, 2007.

Klein, Barrett A., et al. "Sleep deprivation impairs precision of waggle dance signaling in honey bees." *Proceedings of the National Academy of Sciences 107*, no. 52 (December 28, 2010): 22705–22709. Abstract available at http://is.gd/LtaTa6 (accessed June 30, 2011).

Lihoreau, Mathieu, et al. "Trade-off between travel distance and prioritization of high-reward sites in traplining bumblebees." *Functional Ecology* (first published online June 28, 2011). Full text (pdf) available at http://is.gd/zxkMZG (accessed June 30, 2011).

Maeterlinck, Maurice. *The Life of the Bee*. New York: New American Library, Mentor Books, 1954. First published 1901 by Blue Ribbon Books.

Mazar, Amihai, and Nava Panitz-Cohen. "It is the land of honey: Beekeeping in Iron Age IIA Tel Rehov – culture, cult and economy." *Near Eastern Archaeology 70*, no. 44 (2007): 202–219. Full text (pdf) available at http://is.gd/MQsHBz (accessed June 30, 2011).

Münch, David, et al. "In the laboratory and during free-flight: Old honey bees reveal learning and extinction deficits that mirror mammalian functional decline." *PLoS ONE 5*, no. 10 (October 19, 2010): e13504. Full text available at http://is.gd/uXioGW (accessed June 30, 2011).

Savage, Candace Sherk. *Prairie: A Natural History*. Vancouver: David Suzuki Foundation: Greystone Books/Douglas & McIntyre, 2004. [Berkeley, Calif.]: Distributed in US by Publishers Group West.

Schoenherr, Allan A. *A Natural History of California*. Berkeley: University of California Press, 1992.

Seeley, Thomas D. *The Wisdom of the Hive: The Social Physiology of Honey Bee Colonies*. Cambridge, Mass.: Harvard University Press, 1995.

Smith, A.R., et al. "Socially induced brain development in a facultatively eusocial sweat bee, *Megalopta genalis* (*Halicitdae*)." *Proceedings of the Royal Society, Series B*, 277, no. 1691 (July 22, 2010): 2157–2163.

Spano, Nadia, et al. "Chemical characterization of a traditional honey-based Sardinian product: *Abbamele*." *Food Chemistry 108* (2008): 81–85. Full text (pdf) available at http://is.gd/uoyCWL (accessed June 30, 2011).

Tennekes, Henk A., and Ami-Bernard Zillweger. *The Systemic Insecticides: A Disaster in the Making*. Zutphen, Netherlands: ETS, 2010.

van Engelsdorp, Dennis, et al. "A survey of honey bee colony losses in the U.S., fall 2007 to spring 2008." *PLoS ONE 3*, no. 12 (December 30, 2008): e4071. Full text available at http://is.gd/tDZJ7O (accessed June 30, 2011).

von Frisch, Karl. *The Dancing Bees: An Account of the Life and Senses of the Honey Bee*. 1st US ed. New York: Harcourt, Brace, 1955. Originally published as *Aus dem Leben der Bienen*. Berlin, Göttingen, Heidelberg: Springer Verlag, 1953.

Wilson, Edward O. *Sociobiology: The New Synthesis*. Cambridge, Mass.: Belknap Press of Harvard University Press, 1975.

About the Author

Dr. Reese Halter is an Earth doctor, an award-winning science communicator and voice for ecology, a distinguished conservation biologist at California Lutheran University and a broadcaster. He is a sought-after public speaker and founder of the international conservation institute Global Forest Science, through which he regularly visits schools and encourages children worldwide to embrace conservation, science exploration and learning. Dr. Reese and his family live in Malibu, California, and can be contacted through www.DrReese.com.

Other Titles in this Series

The Insatiable Bark Beetle
Dr. Reese Halter
ISBN 978-1-926855-66-0

Ethical Water
Learning To Value What Matters Most
Robert William Sandford
& Merrell-Ann S. Phare
ISBN 978-1-926855-70-7

Becoming Water
Glaciers in a Warming World
Mike Demuth
ISBN 978-1-926855-72-1